W9-BSD-154

Going Around the Sun: Some Planetary Fun

DEDICATIONS

For children everywhere: Be good to Mother Earth.
And for Scott, Melissa, Emily and Elisabeth Broker:
You are my sunshine. — MB

For my husband, Kevin, who looks into the night sky and dreams,
and for Colton, Nathan, and Peyton, who always appear
when I ask for help. And in Memory of Miss Ruby.
— JM (aka NeeNee)

Special thanks to Mrs. Barrett's class at Seminole Springs Elementary School
and Ms. Carrero's class at Palm City Elementary School
featured on the "Tips from the Author" page.

Copyright © 2008 Marianne Berkes
Illustration copyright © 2008 Janeen Mason

A Sharing Nature With Children Book

All rights reserved. No part of this book may be reproduced or transmitted to any form or by any means, electronic or mechanical, including photocopying, recording, or by any information and retrieval system, without written permission from the publisher.

Library of Congress Cataloging-in-Publication Data

Berkes, Marianne Collins.
  Going around the sun : some planetary fun / by Marianne Berkes ; illustrated by Janeen Mason.
    p. cm.
  Summary: "Our Earth is part of a fascinating planetary family: eight planets and an odd bunch of other solar system bodies that spin, roll, tilt, blow and whirl around the Sun. Here, to the tune of 'Over in the Meadow,' young ones can get a glimpse of our remarkable neighborhood"--Provided by publisher.
  ISBN 978-1-58469-099-3 (hardback) -- ISBN 978-1-58469-100-6 (pbk.) 1. Planets--Juvenile literature. 2. Solar system--Juvenile literature. I. Mason, Janeen I., ill. II. Title.
  QB602.B45 2008
  523.4--dc22

                    2007035607

Printed in China
10 9 8 7 6 5 4 3 2 1
First Edition

Computer production by Patty Arnold, Menagerie Design and Publishing.

Dawn Publications
12402 Bitney Springs Road
Nevada City, CA 95959
530-274-7775
nature@dawnpub.com

Going Around the Sun: Some Planetary Fun

by

Marianne Berkes

illustrated by

Janeen Mason

ROUND LAKE AREA
LIBRARY
906 HART ROAD
ROUND LAKE, IL 60073
(847) 546-7060

Dawn Publications

Up in outer space
In a great galaxy,
Lived an old Mother Sun,
And her planet, Mercury.

"Whirl," said the Mother.
"I whirl," said the One.
So it whirled and it twirled
As it went around the Sun.

Mercury, like all the planets, "whirls" or
orbits around the Sun.

Up in outer space
In our sky of pink and blue,
Venus shines a light so bright.
Here is planet number two.

"Sparkle," said the Mother.
"I sparkle," said Two.
So it shined a steady light
In our sky of pink and blue.

Venus "sparkles" brilliantly, but it's not
a star, it's a planet!

Up in outer space
Made of land and of sea,
Is our home planet Earth.
We are planet number three.

"Tilt," said the Mother.
"I tilt," said Three.
So it tilted on its axis
And the seasons came to be!

Earth "tilts" while it goes around
the Sun each year. That causes seasons.

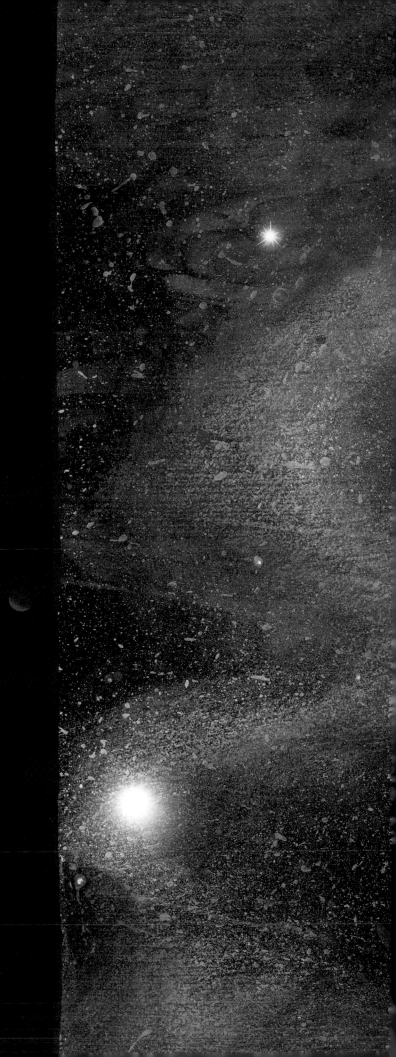

Up in outer space
Filled with iron in its core,
Is the rocky planet Mars.
Here is planet number four.

"Turn," said the Mother.
"I turn," said Four.
So it turned and we learned
There was iron in its core.

Mars "turns" like Earth, but has
huge canyons, craters and volcanoes.

Up in outer space
Planet Jupiter will arrive,
A gigantic ball of gas.
Here is planet number five!

"Spin" said the Mother.
"I spin," said Five.
So it spun around the Sun
And it finally did arrive.

Jupiter, the largest planet, is made
mostly of gas, and "spins" the fastest.

Up in outer space
Where the swirling gases mix,
Is a planet rimmed with rings.
Windy Saturn's number six.

"Blow," said the Mother.
"I blow," said Six.
So it blew and it whirled,
Where the swirling gases mix.

Saturn really "blows"— it has winds
of over 1,000 miles an hour.

Up in outer space
Many moons in its heaven,
Is the planet Uranus.
This is planet number seven.

"Roll," said the Mother.
"I roll," said Seven.
So it leaned and it rolled
In a moon-studded heaven.

Uranus' axis leans so far to one side
that it seems to "roll" through space.

Up in outer space
Mother Sun has to wait,
For the far planet Neptune,
Is a tardy number eight.

"Move," said the Mother.
"I move," said Eight.
So it moved—oh, so slowly
And the Sun had to wait.

Neptune takes 165 Earth-years to go
around the Sun—it needs to "move!"

Up in outer space
Where the planets stay in line,
Mother Sun asked a question,
"Is small Pluto really nine?"

"Pluto," asked the Mother,
"Why can't you stay in line?"
"I am really very different
So I'm not a planet nine."

Tiny Pluto is so different that it is now called
a "dwarf planet."

Up in outer space
There is more that will be told.
There are also smaller bodies
Traveling in the solar fold.

"We zip," said the small ones.
"You zip," said the Sun.
So they zipped and they dipped
And they had a lot of fun.

Lots of other small things "zip"
around the Sun!

Now we know about the planets
That go 'round Mother Sun,
When you name all the planets
Then this far-out journey's done.

OUR FAMILY OF PLANETS

In this story, the Mother Sun and her planets are having a conversation. The Sun, from which the planets get their energy, tells them how to go around her. Of course we know the Sun doesn't talk; that is fiction. But do the planets go around the Sun? Yes, that's a fact.

Each planet goes around, or *orbits*, the Sun. Mother Sun's *gravity* (attractive force) pulls on each planet—sort of like each planet being on a leash, keeping them nearby while they go around her. Each planet *rotates* (spins) on its *axis*, which is an imaginary pole that runs through its center.

The word "solar" refers to the Sun. The Solar System includes the Sun and everything that goes around it. That's our planetary family!

People who study things beyond the Earth are called astronomers. They are always finding out more about the universe. (The word "universe" comes from the Latin word for "whole world.")

Here are some things we already know:

- Our Sun is a star that's only 93 million miles away—much closer than any other star. Stars are spinning balls of hot gases. There are billions of them, in groups called "galaxies."

- Our Solar System "family" of the Sun and eight planets is part of a huge group or galaxy of stars (some of which have planets, too) called the Milky Way.

- The Milky Way Galaxy is just one of over a hundred billion (100,000,000,000) galaxies in the universe.

- Our Sun is huge compared to the eight planets that orbit it.

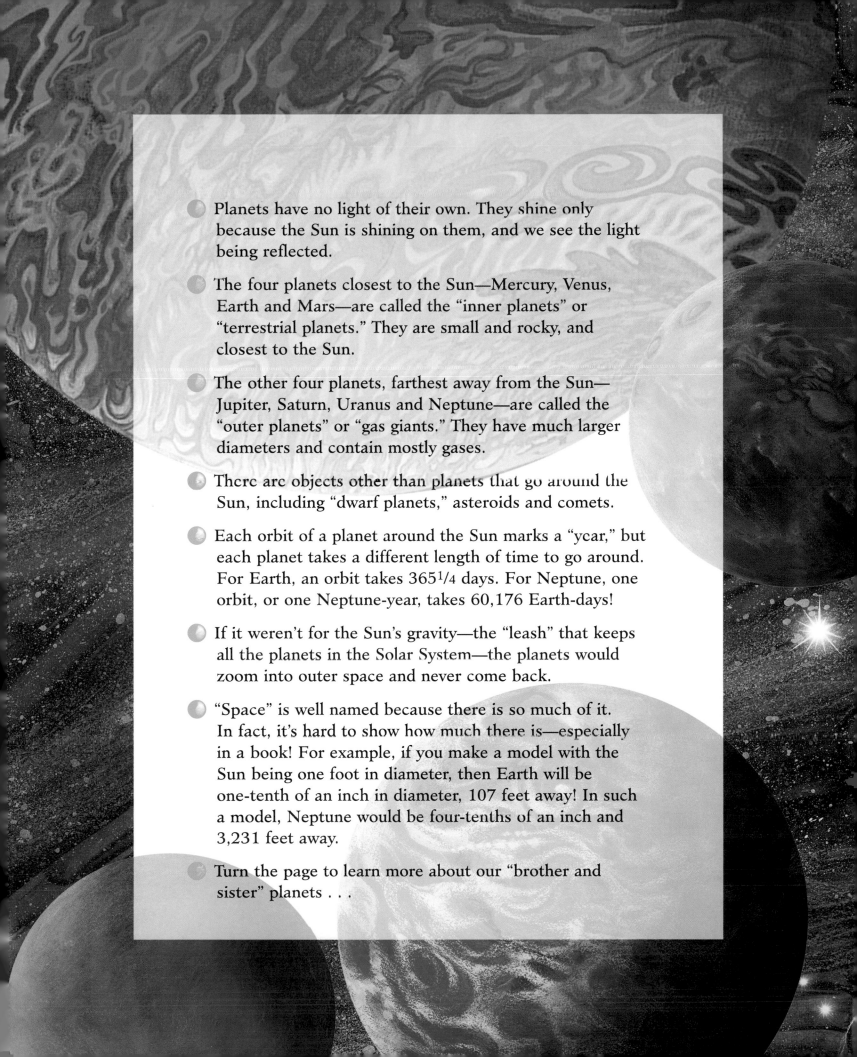

- Planets have no light of their own. They shine only because the Sun is shining on them, and we see the light being reflected.

- The four planets closest to the Sun—Mercury, Venus, Earth and Mars—are called the "inner planets" or "terrestrial planets." They are small and rocky, and closest to the Sun.

- The other four planets, farthest away from the Sun—Jupiter, Saturn, Uranus and Neptune—are called the "outer planets" or "gas giants." They have much larger diameters and contain mostly gases.

- There are objects other than planets that go around the Sun, including "dwarf planets," asteroids and comets.

- Each orbit of a planet around the Sun marks a "year," but each planet takes a different length of time to go around. For Earth, an orbit takes 365 1/4 days. For Neptune, one orbit, or one Neptune-year, takes 60,176 Earth-days!

- If it weren't for the Sun's gravity—the "leash" that keeps all the planets in the Solar System—the planets would zoom into outer space and never come back.

- "Space" is well named because there is so much of it. In fact, it's hard to show how much there is—especially in a book! For example, if you make a model with the Sun being one foot in diameter, then Earth will be one-tenth of an inch in diameter, 107 feet away! In such a model, Neptune would be four-tenths of an inch and 3,231 feet away.

- Turn the page to learn more about our "brother and sister" planets . . .

MERCURY is the smallest planet and is the closest to the Sun. It *whirls* quickly across the sky compared to the other planets. That is probably why it was named after a Roman god who was known as a swift messenger. It is only seen from Earth in the morning or evening twilight sky. Usually the glare of the Sun makes it impossible to see. It's very hot—up to 800 degrees F— and has almost no air. Mercury is rocky, with a crater as large as Texas!

VENUS is named for the Roman goddess of love and beauty because it *sparkles* so brilliantly. It's covered with thick clouds of sulfuric acid. They do not make rain, so Venus is very dry and the hottest planet of all, sometimes over 900 degrees F. The clouds reflect sunlight—and also trap the Sun's heat like a greenhouse. Venus' surface is covered with volcanoes that oozed molten lava.

EARTH'S name comes from an old German word meaning "dirt." From space, our home planet looks like a shiny blue marble because so much of its surface is covered with water. Our Earth has one moon which orbits around it. The pull of gravity from the moon causes Earth's oceans to have tides that rise and fall. Because the Earth is *tilted* on its axis, different parts of the Earth face the Sun more directly as it orbits the Sun, while other parts face the Sun less directly. That causes the seasons.

MARS was named after the Greek god of war because of its reddish color, which comes from iron oxide. Mars has many huge canyons and craters. Two small moons orbit close to Mars. Every time Mars *turns* on its axis, it is another day on Mars. Days on Mars are just 39 minutes longer than days on Earth. Like Earth, Mars also tilts and has seasons. But because it is twice as far from the Sun as Earth, a hot summer day would only be about 50 degrees F, while winter temperatures might be 200 degrees F below freezing.

JUPITER is named after Jove, the chief god of the Romans. The red spot, which has been seen from Earth for about 350 years, is a huge continuing storm. Jupiter is so large in diameter that all the other planets in the solar system could fit inside it. It is made up mostly of swirling gases that change colors often. It *spins* or rotates on its axis faster than any other planet, completing one rotation, or day, in only 10 hours. But it takes Jupiter twelve Earth-years to go around the Sun once. Jupiter has at least 60 moons.

SATURN is named after the Roman god of the harvest. Like Jupiter, it is a giant ball made up mostly of gases. It is most famous for its bright rings, which are made of many ice and rock particles. All four of the "Gas Giants"—Jupiter, Saturn, Uranus and Neptune—have rings, but Saturn's are the brightest and largest. Around Saturn's middle, winds *blow* well over a thousand miles an hour. The white spots on Saturn are believed to be powerful storms. Saturn has 48 named moons and more are being discovered.

URANUS is named after the ancient Greek god of the heavens. It rotates on its side so it may appear to *roll* rather than spin through space. Sometimes its axis points towards the Sun, so that one of its poles faces the Sun for years at a time. There is even a debate among astronomers about which pole is "north" and which is "south." Uranus has at least 20 moons; the average temperature is 357 degrees F below freezing. It takes Uranus eighty Earth-years to orbit the Sun.

NEPTUNE may have been named after the Roman God of the Sea because of its deep blue color. It looks like a little blue dot from Earth. Neptune is the coldest and farthest planet from the Sun, about 30 times farther than Earth. It takes almost 165 Earth-years for Neptune to *move* (or orbit) around the Sun once. Two thick and two thin rings surround Neptune along with eight moons. The largest moon, Triton, is odd in that it orbits in the opposite direction of the other seven moons.

PLUTO, until recently, was the farthest and smallest planet. But in 2006, astronomers decided it should be called a "dwarf planet" instead. They decided that three things must happen for anything to be called a planet. First, it must orbit the Sun. Second, it must be massive enough for its gravity to squish it into a round shape. And third, it must be massive enough for its gravity to attract and clear out other objects in its neighborhood. While Pluto orbits the Sun and is round, it has not cleared other objects out of its neighborhood. In addition, Pluto doesn't *stay in line*—its orbit sometimes brings it closer to the Sun than Neptune.

Smaller objects orbit the Sun too—lots of them. In addition to Pluto, there are currently two other "dwarf planets," Ceres and Eris. Eris is more massive than Pluto. There are quite a few other objects that are candidates to be named as dwarf planets. All objects that are not at least dwarf planets are known as "Small Solar System Bodies." Astronomers put them into various groups such as asteroids (space rocks) and comets (dusty snowballs) depending on their size, location, and other characteristics. Smaller ones are pulled this way and that by the gravity of more massive bodies as they orbit the Sun.

● Tips from the Author

Going Around the Sun offers some wonderful opportunities for extended activities. Here are a few ideas:

Create a play Teachers may want to use this book for a reader's theater. Students can help put the script together with a narrator and ten or more characters. Younger children can also sing this adaptation of "Over in the Meadow" by Olive A. Wadsworth.

Remember their names and positions When Pluto was still considered a planet, one device to remember the names of the planets and their order from the Sun was "My Very Educated Mother Just Sent Us Nine Pizzas." Ask students for their ideas on how to remember it now.

Flannel board story Out of felt, cut a very large Sun and the relative sizes of the eight planets and dwarf planet, Pluto. Place them (or have children do it) on a navy blue or black flannel board as you sing or read the story.

Space Word Wall Discuss the action verb used for each planet, using the glossary as a guide. Write each verb on an index card and place on a poster board. On a larger board, place names of the planets and other nouns like galaxy, axis, etc. Older students can find adjectives and adverbs used in the story as well.

Planet bookmarks Visit my website, www.MarianneBerkes.com, to learn how you can get reproducible bookmarks of the eight different planets.

Plan a model Whether inside the classroom or outside on a playground or in a park, create a model of the planets rotating and revolving around a Sun. Here are three excellent sites for assistance with the numbers:

www.enchantedlearning.com/subjects/astronomy/ planets

www.exploratorium.edu/ronh/solar_system

http://www.planetary.org/explore/kids/activities/ solar_system_model.html

Discover more Here are a few books, web-based resources and organizations:

- ● *Exploring the Solar System with 22 Activities* by Mary Kay Carson (2006)
- ● *The Planets* by Gail Gibbons (Rev. Ed. 2005)
- ● *Solar System* by Mike Goldsmith (2005)
- ● *The Planets in Our Solar System* by Franklyn M. Branley (1998)
- ● *The Planetary Society* has educational games at www.planetary.org/explore/kids/
- ● The NASA Kids Club main page is www.nasa.gov/audience/forkids/home/index.html
- ● The Lunar and Planetary Institute has an education site, www.lpi.usra.edu/education
- ● Check out www.haydenplanetarium.org, and at the American Museum of Natural History's terrific "Ology" site, www.ology.amnh.org/astronomy/

I would love to hear from teachers and parents who come up with other creative ideas on ways to use this book. My website is www.MarianneBerkes.com

Tips from the Illustrator

I was visiting an elementary school in Graceville, Florida when I met an art teacher who grinned, grabbed my arm and hurried me to her big bright art room that smelled like imagination bubbling over. Her kids were making beautiful art by painting with crayons on a warm griddle.

"Exactly what I need to create the illustrations for *Going Around The Sun: Some Planetary Fun*" I said. I raced back to my studio in South Florida with a new pancake griddle under one arm and a great big box of crayons under the other.

I peeled the paper off each crayon and covered the griddle with aluminum foil. Then I turned the dial to "warm." You'll know the temperature is not too hot, and not too cool when your crayons slide across fresh sheets of paper like a whisper.

Day after lovely day I painted the backgrounds for all of the pages in this book with my melted crayons.

I painted clear gesso over all of the melted crayon backgrounds, and with brushes, acrylic gouache, color pencils and a little computer magic I created the planets, star clusters and asteroids layer by layer over each other until I finished the art you see in these pages.

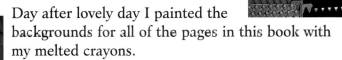

You can paint with melted crayons, too. You'll need a helpful adult, a griddle, some crayons, a little aluminum foil and some fresh paper. Or you could make wax paper planets like this:

Begin by sharpening crayons over a paper plate. Ask an adult to help by heating up an iron. Place your crayon shavings between two sheets of waxed paper and carefully set the iron on the waxed paper for just an instant. The crayon will melt quickly between the two sheets of waxed paper. When it cools you can cut out shapes of the planets and tape them to the inside of your windows or hang them from strings to create your very own solar system. You can visit me at www.JaneenMason.com.

● Also by Marianne Berkes

Marianne Berkes has spent much of her life as a teacher, children's theater director and children's librarian. Because she knows how much children enjoy "interactive" stories, she is the author of six entertaining and educational picture books that make a child's learning relevant. Her books are also inspired by her love of nature. Marianne hopes to open kids' eyes to the magic found in our natural world. She recently retired to spend full time writing as well as visiting schools and presenting at conferences. She is an energetic presenter who involves her audience in "fiction, fact and fun."
Her website is www.MarianneBerkes.com.

Janeen Mason is a well-known fine artist—her work appears in collections worldwide—as well as an author and illustrator of children's books. She's even a member of the prestigious Florida Arts Council. So what does she do to illustrate a book about the planets? She buys a bunch of crayons and a warming griddle! Her unique multi-media style and colorful touch lend themselves perfectly to introduce children to our beautiful solar system. In this book she discovered many things. The giant planets are not solid! A wind storm has raged on Jupiter for hundreds of years! She loves learning—and sharing her excitement with children—both through her art and when visiting schools. She lives in Stuart, Florida. www.JaneenMason.com

Over in the Ocean: In a Coral Reef, illustrated by Jeanette Canyon — With unique and outstanding style, this book portrays the vivid community of creatures that inhabit the ocean's coral reefs. Its many awards include the National Parenting Publications Gold Award.

Over in the Jungle: A Rainforest Rhyme, illustrated by Jeanette Canyon — As with *Over in the Ocean*, each page is meticulously composed of polymer clay, then photographed, showing a rain forest teeming with remarkable animals. Named an "Outstanding Product" by iParenting Media for 2007.

Seashells by the Seashore, illustrated by Robert Noreika — Kids discover, identify, and count twelve beautiful shells that they give to Grandma for her birthday.

Some Other Nature Awareness Books From Dawn Publications

Eliza and the Dragonfly by Susie Caldwell Rinehart, illustrated by Anisa Claire Hovemann, a charming story of a girl and a dragonfly, each experiencing their own metamorphosis. Winner of the 2005 International Reading Assn. award for Best Picture Book.

If You Give a T-Rex a Bone, by Tim Myers, illustrated by Anisa Claire Hovemann, takes you back to ancient habitats that are, well—interesting. Dangerously interesting!

The Habitat Series by Anthony Fredericks, illustrated by Jennifer DiRubbio, features communities of creatures in their own neighborhood: *Under One Rock*, *In One Tidepool*, *Around One Cactus*, *Near One Cattail*, and *On One Flower*.

Dawn Publications is dedicated to inspiring in children a deeper understanding and appreciation for all life on Earth. To view our titles or to order, please visit us at www.dawnpub.com, or call 800-545-7475.